MW01709396

Tasty regions

Provence

RECIPES
Christian Etienne

PHOTOGRAPHS AND STYLING
Sébastien Merdrignac

Editions OUEST-FRANCE

CHICK PEA AND PAPRIKA DIP

Serves 6 to 8

250 g cooked chick peas in brine
2 or 3 cloves garlic
Juice of 2 lemons
1 tablespoon olive oil
1 pinch paprika
1 tablespoon parsley
Chicken stock
Sesame seeds
Chilli to taste
Salt

• Drain the chick peas and blend them in a food processor along with the lemon juice, crushed garlic, seasoning and chicken stock.
• The mixture should not be too thick.
• Reheat gently.
• Serve in a large bowl, sprinkled with paprika and chopped parsley.
• Drizzle with olive oil and sprinkle with toasted sesame seeds.

This dish is perfect served as an appetiser, with slices of toast and a glass of good quality white wine.

TAPENADE

Serves 6 to 8

200 g pitted black olives
50 g anchovy fillets
50 g tuna in oil
100 g pickled capers
1 to 2 spoonfuls of olive oil depending on consistency

- Mash all the ingredients together using a pestle and mortar to create a fine paste.
- At the last minute, add the olive oil.
- Keep in an airtight container.

ANCHOVY FILLETS MARINATED IN WINE

60 fresh anchovies divided into fillets
Banyuls sweet wine

- Cover with sea salt for 1 hour then rinse thoroughly.
- Marinate overnight in Banyuls wine then drain and put in olive oil.

ANCHOVIES MARINATED WITH LEMON AND HERBS

Anchovies or sardines
Juice of 1 lemon
Olive oil
Parsley
Chervil
Chives
Salt
Pepper

- Using only very fresh anchovies, fillet them and arrange them carefully in a dish. Add salt, pepper and the lemon juice.
- Leave for a few minutes, then drizzle with good quality olive oil.
- Add the chopped parsley, chervil and chives.

I haven't given exact quantities for this recipe because you can make as much as you can eat; serve with a few slices of slightly warm toast.
It makes a great appetiser.
You can also use sardines instead of anchovies.

SOUPE AU PISTOU (PESTO SOUP)

Serves 6

100 g large green beans
100 g small white haricot beans
2 or 3 courgettes
100 g carrots
50 g potatoes
100 g large vermicelli
4 very ripe tomatoes
5 cloves garlic
1 bunch of basil leaves
75 g parmesan
250 ml olive oil

• Top and hull the green beans, cut them into short lengths. Dice the courgettes.
• Cook the green beans and white haricot beans in 2.5 litres of water, with salt and pepper added. After 15 minutes, add the carrots and potatoes. After a further 15 minutes, add the courgettes.
• Cook for 15 minutes then add the vermicelli.
• Mash together the tomato pulp, garlic, parmesan and basil leaves, adding the olive oil little by little.
• Pour into the boiling soup.

This soup, originally from Genoa, can be served hot in the autumn as well as cold in the summer. The more tomatoes you use, the more refreshing it will be. Often, a few pieces of bacon rind are added, perfect for using up leftovers that are unlikely to be eaten.
This is a typical Provençal summer dish.

FISH SOUP

Serves 6

3 kg rock fish such as scorpion fish, dory, gilthead bream, monkfish, etc.
1 leek
1 fennel bulb
3 garlic bulbs (cut in half)
1 onion
250 g tomato puree
2 g saffron thyme bay leaves

• Lightly fry the vegetables until they start to brown.
• Add the fish, tomato puree and saffron. Stir well until the fish starts to crumble.
• Add water to cover. Add the thyme and bay leaves. Cook for 2 hours at a medium boil.
• Pass through a strainer (not too fine).
• Add salt and pepper to taste and keep warm. There should be at least 5 litres of soup.
• Serve with toasted croutons and a little rouille sauce.

Some people add grated gruyere cheese, but I must admit that I prefer it without.
This soup takes rather a long time to make, but as it's so delicious, it's worth it ! You can buy all sorts of small fish from your fishmonger for this recipe. There are several types of fish soup: the 'grey' or 'trawled' variety, which is much more expensive but is full of flavour, and the 'red' or 'rock' variety, made with small red fish. This variety is excellent.

MUSSEL SOUP WITH SAFFRON

Serves 10

4 kg mussels
500 ml white wine
2 carrots finely chopped
1 onion finely chopped
2 cloves garlic
1 tomato
1 g saffron
Pepper
Thyme, bay leaves
Olive oil

• Wash the mussels thoroughly. Cook them in the white wine with the thyme and bay leaves until they open. Do not overcook, as this will make them rubbery and dry.
• Remove the flesh from the shells and set aside in a soup tureen.
• Strain the juice, taking care not to include any grit (often it sinks to the bottom of the pan).
• Heat the olive oil in a pan and add the carrots and onions.When they are nicely brown, add the finely chopped garlic followed by the tomato and saffron.
• Taste the mussel juice to check that it is not too salty, then add it to the vegetables. If it is too salty, add more water.
• Bring to the boil and pour it over the mussels.
• Serve with toasted croutons rubbed with garlic or rouille sauce.

The mussels we use in our restaurant often come from Thau lagoon.You can also use farmed mussels for this recipe, which are smaller and sometimes plumper.

CREAM OF LENTIL SOUP

Serves 10

300 g green lentils
1 carrot
1 onion
2 cloves garlic
100 g bacon cut into chunks (lardons)
250 ml whipped cream
Olive oil

• Lightly fry the lardons with a little olive oil. When they are nicely golden, add the lentils, 2.5 litres of water and the vegetables.
• Cook for at least an hour, remove the vegetables and purée them. Adjust the seasoning. Add a few drops of olive oil.
• Just before serving, add the whipped cream and use a hand-held blender to combine well.
• This soup can also be eaten cold. It has a very delicate flavour which, with the addition of the olive oil, tastes fantastic.
• Here we have used Puy lentils, which are very dear to my good friend Régis Marcon, a renowned chef in this region of France. Here in Provence, lentils have always been cooked with bacon and lots of water. The cooking juices would be served as a clear soup to eat with dry bread, and the lentils would be eaten either in a salad or served warm with the bacon.One dish would last all week.
• The recipe I have given you here is the one we use at my restaurant in winter.

SALT COD BRANDADE WITH GARLIC CROUTONS

Serves 6

1 kg salt cod
1 kg cod
1 litre milk
1 litre olive oil
1 garlic bulb
1 baguette
150 g truffles
Salt, pepper

• Soak the salt cod overnight. Poach it in the milk along with the fresh cod, then whisk in some of the olive oil. Drain.
• Using a spatula, stir briskly over a very low heat and add the rest of the olive oil until the mixture forms a smooth paste.
• At the last minute, add the crushed garlic and the truffles, cut into julienne strips.
• Adjust the seasoning (not too much salt).
• Spread on slices of toasted baguette.

Salt cod brandade is one of the great specialities of Nimes. Historically, the inhabitants of Nimes used to trade salt with sailors. They also used to desalinate salt cod in their toilet cisterns!

GAME MEATBALLS

Serves 10

500 g game (such as wild boar or woodcock; cheap cuts will do)
200 g cooked spinach
50 g cooked sorrel
100 g onions
150 to 200 g pork caul
5 juniper berries
Garlic
Thyme
Bay leaves
Sage
1 litre chicken or veal stock

• Cut the meat into small cubes and cook slowly as if you were making a stew in order to make a dry stuffing.
• Combine with the spinach, finely chopped cooked onions, garlic, thyme, sorrel and the crushed juniper berries.
• Form into approx. 30 g meatballs and wrap in the caul.
• Place them in an oven-proof dish and fill half-way with the stock.
• Put the sage and bay leaves on top and cook for a good hour at a low heat, 140 °C (gas 4-5).

HERBY MEATBALLS

Serves 10

400 g cooked spinach
400 g cooked Swiss chard
50 g cooked sorrel
100 g onions finely chopped and cooked
3 cloves garlic crushed
100 g finely chopped streaky bacon
200 g well-rinsed pork caul
Thyme
Bay leaves
Sage
1 litre chicken or veal stock

• Combine all the ingredients in a good-sized dish. Season well with salt and pepper.
• Form into approx. 110 g balls wrapped in the caul. Place them in an oven-proof dish. Fill up to the half-way point with the stock.
• Scatter with the thyme, bay leaves and sage and cook for 2 hours at a low heat, 130 to 140°C (gas 4-5).

TOMATO TARTARE WITH HERBS AND RAW SHALLOTS, OLIVE-OIL VINAIGRETTE

Serves 6

10 big tomatoes
1 shallot
1 bunch of basil
Maussane olive-oil
Salt
Pepper
Balsamic vinegar

• Blanch and peel the tomatoes, cut them into quarters and remove the pips. Press them for as long as possible. Rehydrate them with olive oil.
• Season with salt and pepper, and add the chopped basil and thinly cut shallot plus several drops of balsamic vinegar.
• To present, put into round moulds and sprinkle with olive oil just before serving.

• This is a very simple dish. By pressing the tomatoes over-night, all their excess water disappears. When they are rehydrated with a fine quality olive oil, their flavour is even more delicate and pleasing, especially when well-ripened tomatoes have been selected.

I advise drinking a Côtes-du-Rhône 100% Viognier from M. Français (Château Saint- Estève d'Uchaux).

SARDINE TART WITH OVEN-DRIED TOMATOES

Serves 6

1 round tin 30 cm diameter
500 g very fresh sardines
300 g puff pastry
Fresh thyme leaves
Olive oil
Salt, pepper

Oven-dried tomatoes
300 g tomatoes
Fresh thyme leaves
Sugar
Garlic cloves
Olive oil

• Roll out the puff pastry and line the tin. Bake blind using dried haricot beans to keep it flat. Remove beans and cook completely until golden.
• Meanwhile, cut the sardines into fillets. Drain well on a cloth.
• When the pastry base is cooked, leave it to cool a little before arranging the tomatoes on it. Arrange the sardines with the tails facing upwards.
• Add salt and pepper, sprinkle with the thyme leaves, drizzle with olive oil and cook in a hot oven, 170 to 180 °C (gas 5-6) for 10 mins.
• Prepare the oven-dried tomatoes: use Roma plum tomatoes if possible. They should be bright red, ripe, but not too soft.Cut them in half, remove the seeds and spread them out on a baking tray with plenty of space between each one.
• Add salt and pepper, sprinkle on a little sugar, flavour with thyme leaves and add a few crushed garlic cloves.
• Drizzle with olive oil and bake for 4 hours at 100 °C (gas 3-4).
• Chill for a few days.

The tart can be served hot, with a glass of Laudun white wine from the Quatre-Chemins winery. It's a real pleasure. Don't worry about making too much, because if any is left over, it's just as delicious cold.
The sardines are also excellent grilled, served with a mustard sauce. We recommend that you cook this recipe outdoors, as the smell of grilled sardines can be unpleasant if it lingers in the house! Here, the local fishermen eat them grilled without gutting them first, simply rinsing them in running water to remove the scales. Since they only eat the flesh from the back, leaving the innards intact adds a delicious flavour.

SAVOURY CHICKEN LIVER FLAN

Serves 6 to 8

200 g chicken livers
6 eggs
1 litre pouring cream
2 shallots
1 clove garlic
Nutmeg
Salt
Pepper

• Blend all the ingredients together in a food processor. Ensure the livers do not become too warm or oxygenated; blend in several batches.
• Season with 10 g salt, 3 g pepper and a little grated nutmeg. Pass through a fine strainer. The mixture should be liquid.
• Lightly butter the insides of dariole moulds. Fill them with the mixture and cook in a bain-marie at 180 °C (gas 6) for 2 hours.
• Leave to cool then place in the refrigerator for three days. This length of time is needed for the flavours to blend together and develop.

RED MULLET WITH THICK BLACK-OLIVE SAUCE

Serves 6

6 red mullet of 200 to300g (6 to 9 oz) each
300 g (9 oz) black olives
25 cl (1/2 pint) Noilly Prat
25 cl (1/2 pint) fresh cream
200 g (6 oz) butter olive oil

• Remove the bones from the red mullets.
• Blanch the olives and cook them with the Noilly Prat and a little of the cream. Mix. Sieve and add the butter to thicken.
• Fry the red mullet quickly in olive oil.
• The difficulty with this recipe is preparing the fillets. If you are among friends and they don't mind eating with their fingers, leave the bones and simply enjoy yourselves.
• For the sauce, it is advisable to choose Greek olives rather than those of Nyons, since they are not so oily.

I advise drinking a white wine from the Luberon as accompaniment, Château La Verrerie or Val Joanis.

GRATIN OF SCORPION FISH WITH POTATOES

Serves 6

6 scorpion fish fillets weighing 100 g to 120 g
6 good quality firm potatoes (120 to 150 g per person)
100 g pitted black olives
200 g raw tomato dice
1 onion
5 cloves garlic
Olive oil
Fish stock
Flour
Thyme
Bay leaves
Salt, pepper

• Sweat the finely chopped onion in a large gratin dish with the olive oil until it starts to brown.
• Meanwhile, slice the potatoes very thinly (slightly thicker than crisps) and toss the scorpion fish fillets in flour.
• Pan-fry them quickly over a high heat until they start to brown, taking care not to cook them. Place them in the dish.
• In a large bowl, combine the tomatoes, half the olives, potatoes, thyme, bayleaf and crushed garlic. Cover the fish with this mixture as if you were making boulangère potatoes. Arrange the potatoes on top then cover with the fish stock up to the top of the dish. Sprinkle with the rest of the olives.
• Bake in a hot oven, 180 °C (gas 6), for 30 to 40 mins. Crush a potato to test whether it is cooked.

Serve piping hot with a dry white Côtes-du-Rhône.

Scorpion fish is very flavoursome. I would advise you to always buy it in fillets as it has a very big head which means there is a lot of waste. However, you could always make a stock from the head and the bones, which you could then use as liquid for your gratin.

GRILLED TUNA ON A BED OF MIXED PAN-FRIED PEPPERS

Serves 6

6 tuna steaks
1 red pepper
1 yellow pepper
1 green pepper
1 large onion, finely chopped
1 clove garlic
Balsamic vinegar
Olive oil
Salt

• Dice the peppers and blanch them in salted water. Refresh in cold water.
• Lightly fry the onions with a little olive oil, add the peppers and the crushed garlic.
• Brown slightly.
• Grill the tuna steaks, taking care not to over cook them as stuna quickly becomes dry.
• Arrange them on top of the peppers.
• Drizzle with vinaigrette.

• This dish is perfect served with a good Tavel wine from the Roudil family.
• It is often said that tuna is the sea's steak. It is certainly true that the red-flesh varieties could be mistaken for meat. Ask your fishmonger to cut steaks 3 to 4 cm thick, each weighing 130 to 150 g depending on your appetite.

BOUILLABAISSE ("FISH STEW")

Serves 10

Fish soup
3 kg (6 lbs) "red soup"
1 leek
1 fennel root
3 garlic heads (cut in half)
1 onion
250 g (8 oz) tomato concentrate
Thyme
Bay leaves
A generous pinch of saffron

Fish
5 average red mullets (200 g: 6 oz each)
2 John Dory fillets (500 g: 1 lb. each)
cut into 10 portions
5 weevers (100 g: 3 oz each)
1 small conger eel (cut into pieces of about 80 g: 2 1/2 oz each),
5 average scorpion fish – rascasses
(200 g: 6 oz each)
5 red gurnets (200 g: 6 oz each)

Rouille
2 egg yolks
50 cl (1 pint) olive oil
3 cloves of garlic
A pinch of saffron
Paprika, salt and cayenne pepper

Other ingredients
200 g (6 oz) of grated cheese
1 baguette for croûtons
A few rate type potatoes boiled in water
slightly perfumed with saffron for the garnish

Fish soup
• Let the vegetables sweat without browning them. Add the fish (red soup), the tomato concentrate, the saffron. Mix thoroughly until the fish disintegrates.
• Add water to cover.
• Cook for 3 hours on moderate heat. Then sieve (not too fine a sieve).
• Season with salt and pepper and keep warm. There should be at least 5 litres (10 pints) of soup.

Fish
• Take three wide frying pans. Put the red gurnets and the weevers in one; in another the rascasses and the red mullets; and the conger eel and the John Dory in the third.
• Sprinkle the fish with olive oil and a little salt.
• Then moisten half way up with the soup and begin to cook the fish. Once cooked, keep them warm.

Rouille
• Crush the garlic finely then add the egg-yolks, a pinch of saffron, paprika, salt and cayenne pepper.
• Add the oil, mixing gently as for a mayonnaise.
• Soften with a soup-spoon of slightly reduced fish soup.

To serve
• First of all serve the remaining soup with the croûtons, the cheese and the rouille.
• Next, present all the fish on a single platter with a little of the broth.

CUTTLEFISH STUFFED WITH CEPS

Serves 4 to 6

200 to 300 g small cuttlefish
500 g ceps
20 g powdered porcini
500 g mushrooms
3 shallots
2 cloves garlic
10 g fresh parsley
Olive oil
Salt, pepper

• Cut the ceps into small cubes and sauté them in oil with salt and pepper. Drain in a sieve.
• Make a duxelles with the mushrooms (i.e. chop finely).
• Pan-fry the finely-chopped shallots with a little olive oil. When they are nicely brown, add the mushrooms and cook until dry.
• Leave to cool and combine the ceps, duxelles, powdered porcini, finely chopped garlic and parsley.
• Adjust the seasoning, and the stuffing is ready.
• Clean the cuttlefish. Pull the head to release the innards and tentacles. Discard the innards and rinse the tentacles thoroughly. Drain and dry slightly on a tray.
• Cut the tentacles off at eye level (discard the eyes) and chop roughly. Pan-fry and mix with the stuffing.
• Stuff the cuttlefish using a piping bag and nip together with a cocktail stick.
• Pan-fry over a high heat until coloured on both sides. Finish in a hot oven for a few minutes.

Small cuttlefish are delicious as a starter or a main course. Preparing them requires a little time and effort. Here is my recipe for cuttlefish stuffed with ceps, a very tasty dish.
You can serve them as they are with a small salad and a nice herb vinaigrette, or with a crab coulis and some parmesan shavings.

MONKFISH TAIL IN BREADCRUMBS WITH ITS AÏOLI SAUCE

Serves 2

1 tail of monkfish of 800 gm to 1 kg (1 1/2 to 2 lbs)
300 g (10 oz) breadcrumbs
20 g (3/4 oz) thyme flowers
Olive oil
6 cloves of garlic
2 eggs
100 g (3 oz) butter

• Skin and trim the monkfish, insert several cloves of garlic and cover it with breadcrumbs mixed with thyme flowers.
• Cook gently in olive oil and butter.
• Cook in the oven at 180°C, basting often with the olive oil and butter.
• For the sauce, crush the garlic with a pestle and mortar and a pinch of coarse salt.
• When the paste is thick and smooth, add the egg yolks.
• Incorporate the olive oil little by little.
• Continue adding until the desired quantity is obtained.
• Take the monkfish out of the oven, and put it in a serving dish. The aïoli sauce is served separately.
• One can also prepare this recipe with small tails of monkfish, counting one per person. This fish can be accompanied by any boiled vegetable, such as potatoes, carrots and celery hearts.

I advise drinking a white Côtes-du-Rhône Villages (at least two years old) with this dish; Château Saint-Roch from M. Verda (Laudun).

RABBIT WITH HERBS

Serves 6 to 8

1 half-rabbit (saddle + 2 thighs)
10 cloves garlic (not peeled)
200 g (6 oz) pickled tomatoes
5 artichoke hearts (cut into 8)
Thyme, bay, sage
Olive oil
Salt
Pepper

• Preheat oven (200 to 210°C).
• Place rabbit in a baking dish large enough to contain rabbit and all herbs. Pour a good quantity of olive oil over rabbit and place in oven until browned on all sides.
• After 5 to 10 minutes (ensure that rabbit is well browned), roll rabbit in aluminium foil to protect it and put all herbs in the bottom (do not add tomatoes as they are already cooked).
• Put back in oven at a lower temperature. Turn occasionally and stir herbs so that they release their full flavour.
• Cook for a further 5 to 10 minutes then remove rabbit from oven and leave to rest. Ensure that garlic and artichokes are well cooked then remove and degrease dish. Add a few drops of water to make a gravy.
• Add tomatoes, garlic and artichokes.
• Cut saddle in four, thighs in half. Serve piping hot.

SADDLE OF RABBIT WITH PISTOU

Serves 6

3 boned saddles of rabbit salted and peppered and rolled in their "panoufles" with a sprig of rosemary,
1 onion
10 basil leaves
4 cloves of garlic
25 cl (1/2 pint) white wine
2 grains of coriander
1 bouquet garni
30 to 50 g (1 to 1 1/2 oz) butter
Salt
Pepper

• Sauté the saddles in a thick-bottomed frying pan, with their bones and the onion.
• Cook in a very hot oven for 15 to 20 minutes.
• Once they are cooked, take them out and let them rest.
• Degrease the frying pan, add the white wine and an equal amount of water to the bones.
• Add the bouquet garni, the garlic and the coriander.
• Cook gently until the liquid is reduced by half.
• Sieve this gravy, add the butter little by little and the basil at the last minute.
• Cut the saddles in half.
• One can serve this dish with white coco-beans or French beans.

This is a most refreshing dish, and quick to prepare. It is full of flavour.
A red Côtes-du- Rhône, Coteau-des-Baux, or a Château Romanin accompanies it very well.

JUGGED HARE

Serves 6 to 8

1 hare
1 litre good red wine
(Gigondas or Châteauneuf-du-Pape)
2 carrots
2 onions
6 cloves garlic
1 stick celery
3 cloves
6 juniper berries
3 tablespoons flour
Thyme
Bay leaves
Olive oil
Salt, pepper
Garnish
150 g small silverskin onions
150 g diced bacon (lardons)
200 g mushrooms

• Cut the hare into fairly large pieces, reserve the liver having removed the gall bladder, and keep any blood which is inside.
• Marinate the pieces with the onions, carrots, cubed celery, garlic, cloves, juniper berries, thyme and bay leaves. Add enough wine to cover. Leave to marinate for a day in the refrigerator.
• The following day, drain the pieces and reserve the marinade.
• Prepare a good-sized saucepan and fry the vegetables in olive oil. Brown the pieces of hare in a frying pan. Place them in the saucepan with the vegetables.
• Add the flour, stir well, add the marinade, salt, pepper and cook for 2 hours over a low heat.
• Meanwhile, finely chop the liver and combine it with the remaining blood.
• After cooking, remove the pieces, taste the sauce and adjust the seasoning.
• If the sauce is a little acidic, cook for a few more minutes.
• Prepare a garnish with: 150 g small silverskin onions, lightly cooked and browned; 150 g diced bacon (lardons), blanched and sautéed until crisp; 200 g mushrooms, cut into quarters, the same width as the small onions.
• Add this garnish to the pieces of hare.
• At the last minute, add the liver and blood to the sauce, which should bind it together and create a rich black colour. Pour over the pieces of hare and heat gently.
• Note: do not allow it to boil, as the blood will form granules and the dish will not be as good.
• Serve this marvellous dish with steamed potatoes or fresh pasta.

The best hares for cooking are known as 'trois-quarts' ('three-quarters'), i.e. under a year old. They weigh between 2.5 and 3 kg. But, for this recipe, 'capu- cins' (hares over a year old weighing 4 to 5 kg) work very well and can even be better.

ROAST PARTRIDGE WITH KALE CHARTREUSE

Serves 4

2 partridges
1 kale
2 onions
2 carrots
100 g diced bacon (lardons)
5 cloves garlic

• Cut the kale into quarters. Remove the stalk and reserve the green leaves. Braise the white leaves with the finely chopped onions and carrots and the fried bacon.
• Bake in the oven for 2 hours at 130-150 °C (gas 4-5).
• Roast the partridge with the cloves of garlic for 5 mins on each side and 5 mins on the back. Leave the partridges to rest for at least ten minutes, remove the bones, reserve the meat in the fatty juices produced during cooking. The thighs may be a little pink, so grill them slightly.
• Crush the carcass and use it to make gravy by frying it then adding water to cover. Cook until semi-reduced, pass through a fine strainer and put to one side.
• Meanwhile, make the kale chartreuse using a small circular mould, 5 cm diameter and 3 to 4 cm high. Line the moulds with green kale leaves. Braise and re-cook in the oven for 30 mins at 150 to 160 °C (gas 5-6).
• Arrange the partridge meat in the centre of the serving dish or plates with the thighs at the side, surrounded by the hot gravy.

LEG OF DUCK WITH CEPS

Serves 6

6 duck legs
1.5 kg ceps
1 shallot
2 cloves garlic
500 ml chicken or veal stock
150 g butter parsley
Salt, pepper

• Fry the duck legs in a casserole.
• Ensure they are nicely brown on both sides. Remove any fat which has risen to the surface and add the finely chopped shallot and garlic.
• When nicely browned, add the stock and cook until completely reduced.
• Sauté the ceps in a frying pan, then drain. Reserve any cooking juices. Fry once again. Add salt and pepper. They should become golden.
• Add the cooking juices from the ceps to the duck legs in the casserole.
• Reduce again by half and incorporate the butter.
• Add the ceps at the last minute, along with the chopped parsley.
• Re-heat thoroughly, and enjoy with a glass of Gigondas.

GUINEA FOWL SUPREME STUFFED WITH FOIE GRAS

Serves 4

4 slices breast of guinea fowl from Drôme
200 g (6 oz) foie gras
Salt, pepper
1 glass port
1 litre (2 pints) chicken stock
1 onion
3 cloves garlic
1 carrot
100 g (3 oz) butter

• Flatten slices of breast. Remove the small nerve running through the fillets.
• Cut wings to remove all bones (set aside for sauce).
• Flatten fillets to make escalopes that are not too thin. Season with salt and pepper.
• Cut foie gras into four equal pieces (50 g or 1 1/2 oz each). Roll them slightly to form a sausage shape. Wrap escalope round foie gras and roll tightly in clingfilm.
• Poach, in clingfilm, for 30 to 40 minutes depending on size, in stock. N.B. Do not allow to boil.
• Meanwhile, make gravy with wings. Fry until golden with all trimmings in a large saucepan. When wings are golden brown, add onions, garlic and diced carrots and cook until golden. Be careful not to burn the juices that run from meat and vegetables.
• Degrease and deglaze with glass of port. Reduce then pour in enough stock to cover bones. Cook for 30 minutes, skimming to remove any impurities that float up to the surface. Strain the gravy and reduce again by half over a low heat.
• The fillets will now be cooked. Remove clingfilm and place fillets on a large serving dish.
• At the last minute, check the gravy, correct seasoning and gently blend in 100 g (3 oz) butter. Pour over fillets.

This dish can be eaten with boiled rice or spelt.

ROAST LOIN OF LAMB WITH COURGETTES AND TOMATOES

Serves 6

2 loins (carrés) of lamb of 1 to 1.2 kg each - about 2 lbs each (it is a good idea to ask your butcher if you can keep the bones when he prepares them, since you can use these for the gravy)
6 courgettes
8 tomatoes
3 onions
8 cloves of garlic
Thyme, bay leaves

• Prepare a gravy with the lamb bones: brown them in the oven, and then put them in the casserole with garlic, onion, thyme and bay leaves.
• Cook gently for 2 hours, then sieve and reduce again, skimming all the time.
• Meanwhile, prepare the vegetables. Slice the courgettes and the tomatoes thinly. Place the courgettes and the tomatoes in an oven-proof dish on a bed of chopped onions sprinkled with thyme, bay leaves and crushed garlic, layer by layer.
• Pour over a little olive oil and place in a hot oven (150 to 160°C - about 320°F) for 2 hours, covered with foil and a lid so that all the flavours mix together.
• An hour before the meal, cook the lamb till it is pink, 20 minutes in a very hot oven is quite enough (180 to 200°C - about 380°F).
• Let the meat stand a little, and then reheat it slightly before serving with the courgettes and tomatoes, using your tasty gravy to moisten everything.

DAUBE À L'AVIGNONNAISE (AVIGNON-STYLE CASSEROLE)

Serves 6

1 leg of lamb, boned
8 to 10 lardons
Marinade
100 ml olive oil per litre of wine red wine
3 carrots
5 onions
6 cloves garlic
1 bunch parsley
250 g bacon fresh rind dried orange peel
Thyme
Bay leaves
Salt, pepper

• Cut the boned leg of lamb into cubes, weighing about 90 g each.
• Make a cut in each piece following the direction of the meat and insert a lardon in each, seasoned with spiced salt.
• Marinate the pieces for 2 hours with 100 ml of oil per litre of wine, the finely chopped carrots and onions, four cloves of garlic, thyme, bay leaves and parsley.
• Chop three onions and combine with two crushed cloves of garlic. Blanch 250 g bacon cut into small cubes.
• Cut 250 g fresh bacon rind into 2 cm cubes and blanch.
• Prepare a bunch of parsley wrapped around the dried orange peel.
• Line the base and sides of a terrine dish with the thin bacon rashers, and arrange the pieces of lamb in layers, alternating with the onions, bacon and rind, sprinkling each layer of meat with powdered bay leaves and thyme.
• Place the parsley in the middle of the terrine and season each layer as you go.
• Pour over the strained marinade, close the terrine, fasten the lid with string in f order to concentrate the steaming process.
• Start cooking on the hob, then bake in the oven for 5 hours at a low heat, equally distributed throughout cooking.
• Just before serving, uncover the terrine, remove the rashers, skim off any fat and remove the parsley.
• The daube can be served just as it is, straight from the dish.

This is a rather time-consuming recipe that would originally be cooked in the fireplace, but if you're prepared to take the time to make it and have a passion for dishes in rich sauces, this recipe is well worth it.

TROTTERS AND PACKETS

Serves 10

12 little lamb packets (paquets)
6 sheep's trotters
1 pepper
1.2 kg (2 1/2 lbs) neck of lamb
1 kg (2 lbs) tomatoes
200 g (6 oz) carrots
300 g (9 oz) onions
1 litre (2 pints) white wine

• The packets are made of lamb tripes cut into triangles, stuffed with a big lump of salted pork and a parsley, garlic and bread-crumbs mixture (persillade), rolled and tied with string. Personally, I would advise you to ask your tripe butcher to do this.
• Let the vegetables sweat in a little olive oil. When they are well coloured, add the trotters and then the packets on top.
• Add the tomatoes last, with salt, pepper and pimento.
• Moisten with 2 pints of good white wine and complete with water if necessary. Cook for 6 hours in a slow oven. Once cooked, remove the packets and trotters.
• Re-cook the gravy so that it is no longer acid. This dish is served very hot with boiled potatoes.

I advise drinking a light Côtes-du-Rhône red wine: Domaine de la Remejeanne from M. and Mme. Klein, wine-growers who are as enthusiastic as myself.
This is a splendid Provençal recipe. There is always a celebration when someone in the family prepares this dish. It is often a pretext for inviting friends, since it is a meal meant for sharing.

BEEF CHEEK

Serves 6

1.2 kg beef cheek
100 g carrots
100 g onions
200 g shallots
150 g silverskin onions
150 g mushrooms
150 g garlic
1 litre Châteauneuf-du-Pape wine flour
Bouquet garni

• De-vein the beef cheeks and trim off any fat, then seal in a frying pan. Reserve.
• Brown the carrots cut into strips along with the finely chopped onions, shallots and garlic bulbs cut in half.
• Add the beef cheeks then sprinkle with flour.
• Pour in the Châteauneuf-du-Pape and add enough water to cover, add the bouquet garni then place in the oven for 4 hours at 150 °C (gas 5).
• Remove the pieces of meat after cooking, strain the sauce then reduce down to a fairly thick consistency.
• Brown the onions, sauté the mushrooms and add them to the sauce.
• Heat through and pour over the meat.

This dish can be served with home-made mashed potatoes or pasta as the sauce is very highly flavoured. It is excellent with a Châteauneuf-du-Pape.

PROVENÇAL TOMATOES

Serves 4

8 very ripe tomatoes
50 g garlic
1 bunch flat-leaf parsley
150 g white breadcrumbs
Olive oil
Fresh thyme leaves
Salt
Pepper

- Pre-heat the oven to 150-160 °C (gas 5-6).
- Chop the garlic and parsley.
- Cut the tomatoes in half. Squash them firmly to remove the seeds.
- Place them on an oven tray or in a gratin dish. Season with salt and pepper, sprinkle with thyme leaves.
- Mix the parsley and garlic with a little olive oil and the breadcrumbs to create a thick, oily paste.
- Coat the tomatoes with this paste and bake in the oven at 150-160 °C (gas 5-6).
- Cook for 20 to 30 mins.

I like them nicely cooked but not shrivelled up as some people prefer. I like it when they are still juicy in the middle. Provençal tomatoes should be eaten hot accompanied by a well-chilled rosé. Simple and delicious!
There are thousands of recipes for Provençal tomatoes. Mothers and grand-mothers everywhere each have their own favourites. Each family and each household has a different version and everyone swears that theirs is not only the most authentic but also the best, and of course they are all right!

ROUND COURGETTES FROM NICE STUFFED WITH FRAGRANT MARJORAM

Serves 6

6 round courgettes weighing 80 to 100 g
1 chopped onion
2 chopped cloves garlic
30 g marjoram
2 egg yolks
2 tablespoons double cream olive oil

• Cut off the top third of the courgette. Scoop out the flesh with a spoon (carefully, so as not to pierce the skin). Blanch in salted water, along with the courgette lids. Meanwhile, sweat the onion with a little olive oil.
• When it begins to go transparent, add the courgette flesh and the garlic, and cook gently until dry. Stir often until it forms a purée. Add the cream. Continue to reduce a little, almost by half. Leave to cool, mix in the egg yolks, adjust the seasoning. Add the chopped marjoram. Dry the courgette shells with a cloth or kitchen paper, and fill with the stuffing.
• Place the lids on top and bake in the oven at 160 °C (gas 5-6). Drizzle with oil and bake slowly for 2 to 2.5 hours. The stuffing is cooked when it has the consistency of egg custard.

Serve hot with a herb vinaigrette, or cold if you prefer. They are also delicious served with large cuts of meat such as rib of beef.

RAGOÛT OF SNOW PEAS WITH BACON

Serves 8 to 10

1 kg (2 lbs) snow peas (mangetout)
100 g (3 oz) diced fresh bacon
2 onions
4 cloves of garlic
50 cl (1 pint) beef stock or water
5 cl (1/10 pint) olive oil
50 g (1 1/2 oz) pickled tomatoes
Salt
Pepper

• Brown the bacon and chopped onions in the olive oil.
• Add the garlic and snow peas with 1 pint of beef stock and cook gently for 10 minutes.
• Season with salt and pepper.
• Arrange the mixture in a circle and pour the reduced beef stock in the centre, with the diced pickled tomatoes around the edge.
• Previously, green vegetables were cooked in large quantities of water; snow peas and spinach for example. These days, it is more usual to braise them gently so that they give their own juice and remain aromatic. The result is better, and the vitamins are conserved as well.

I suggest drinking a Châteauneuf-du-Pape or a red Bandol.

ARTICHOKE BARIGOULE

Serves 6

12 purple artichokes
2 carrots
2 onions
1 garlic bulb
1 stick celery
1 bunch of basil leaves
Olive oil
Thyme bay leaves
Chicken or veal stock

• Cut out the artichoke hearts, keep the white leaves.
• Fry the carrots, onions and celery together.
• Fry the finely chopped white leaves.
• Stuff the artichoke hearts. Braise them in the stock with the roughly chopped garlic, thyme and bay leaf.
• Cook for 20 to 30 mins depending on size. Remove the hearts.
• Reduce the sauce. Add the chopped basil. Adjust the seasoning.

This is a truly Mediterranean vegetable dish. It apparently originates from Sicily. We have Catherine de Medici to thank for bringing it to us! The type of artichokes used here are the purple variety or baby artichokes which we eat raw with a little sea salt and olive oil.

RATATOUILLE

Serves 8

6 courgettes
2 onions
3 green peppers
6 tomatoes
3 cloves of garlic
4 aubergines
1 big bouquet garni

- Cut the courgettes into cubes without peeling them.
- Peel and slice up the onions.
- Empty the peppers and dice them.
- Peel, remove the pips and cut the tomatoes into quarters.
- Crush the garlic.
- Strip the aubergines and cut them into big cubes.
- Fry the aubergines and courgettes in a frying pan, put them in a colander for their oil to drip.
- Blanch the peppers in plenty of water.
- Let the onions sweat in a little oil and almost brown them.
- Mix everything together (onions, tomatoes, aubergines, courgettes, peppers and the garlic last).
- Add the bouquet garni and bring to the boil.
- Add salt and pepper, and it's ready.

Ratatouille, the famous Provençal recipe, can be eaten hot or cold. It is traditional not to peel the vegetables since the skin adds flavour and the vegetables do not end up as a purée. Evidently, it is advisable to wash them well and to use fresh products from the markets of Provence.

PINE-KERNEL TART

Serves 6 to 8

Tart base in sweet pastry
100 g (3 oz) sugar
100 g (3 oz) butter
400 g (12 oz) pine kernels
25 cl (1/2 pint) double cream

- Prepare a light brown caramel with the butter. Add the pine kernels.
- Let them cook and then add the cream to make a sauce. Pour into the tart base. Cook in the oven.
- This is a very typical Provençal recipe; the pine kernels can be replaced by chopped almonds, and the tart remains soft for at least two days.

I suggest drinking a vintage Muscat de Beaumes-de-Venise with this, coming from the cooperative cellars.

OREILLETTES ("WEET PASTRY FRITTERS")

Serves 6

1 kg flour
40 g sugar
3 grated oranges
2 grated lemons
10 ml groundnut oil
Juice of half an orange
125 g melted sugar
3 eggs
Icing sugar

• Mix together the flour, sugar, eggs, orange juice, and lemon and orange zest to form a smooth paste. Incorporate the melted butter.
• Roll out the paste very thinly. Cut into triangles and fry in very hot oil.
• Drain on kitchen paper.
• Once cooked and drained, sprinkle with icing sugar.

PROVENÇAL NAVETTES ("BOBBINS")

Serves 20 navettes

750 g (1 1/2 lbs) flour
375 g (3/4 lb) caster sugar
65 g (2 oz) butter
The zest of 1 lemon
3 eggs
10 cl (1/5 pint) water
Salt

• Make a well in the flour and add the sugar, the softened butter, the lemon zest, a pinch of salt and the eggs.
• Incorporate the water to obtain a smooth mixture.
• Form little sausage shapes depending on the required size of the navettes.
• Cut them into sections and make them oval in shape.
• Place them on a buttered baking sheet.
• Nick the centre of each navette.
• Leave them to stand for 1 hour.
• Brush them with egg yolk and then put them in a moderate oven.
• Take them out when they are brown.

CROQUANTS ("CRUNCHIES")

Serves 8 to 10

400 g (12 oz) flour
250 g (8 oz) whole almonds (with the skin)
125 g (4 oz) icing sugar
4 eggs
Salt

- Mix the flour, sugar and almonds. Stir in the eggs.
- Roll little sausages about 20 mm (nearly 1 inch) in diameter.
- Cook in the oven at 180°C (350°F) for 15 minutes. Cut into rounds when they are still hot.

A dry cake to be eaten at coffee-time or as a snack, a cake which grandmothers always keep in their cupboards.

POMPE À HUILE OR FOUGASSE ("SWEET FLATBREAD")

Serves 6

125 g + 325 g flour
150 g sugar
100 ml olive oil
1 orange
1 lemon
20 g fresh yeast
1 egg yolk
2 tablespoons orange blossom essence

- The day before, prepare the leaven with 125 g flour, the yeast and 80 ml water.
- Leave to rest overnight.
- The following day, grate the orange and lemon zest. Place 325 g of flour in a large bowl and make a well in the centre. Pour in the sugar, salt, oil and orange blossom essence. Mix with the leaven to form a smooth dough. Leave to rest for approx. 30 mins.
- Beat the dough well on the worktop to remove all the fermenting gases.
- Roll out to a width of 1 cm. Cut into rectangles and put slits in the middle with a knife.
- Bake in the oven at 180 °C (gas 6) for 20 mins.

This excellent Provençal recipe is always served traditionally at Christmas.

ICED NOUGAT WITH HONEY FROM PROVENCE

Serves 4

125 g (4 oz) sliced almonds
50 g (1 1/2 oz) hazelnuts
25 g (3/4 oz) pistachio nuts
200 g (6 oz) sugar
100 g (3 oz) sultanas
75 cl (1 1/2 pints) whipped cream
350 g (11 oz) honey
75 g (2 oz) glucose
250 g (8 oz) egg whites

• Grill the almonds, hazelnuts and pistachios.
• Make a caramel with 150 gm (4 1/2 oz) sugar, and add the almonds. Turn on to a plate to cool.
• Reduce to a powder, then grind up the hazelnuts and pistachios and add them.
• Whip up the cream till it holds.
• Make the honey meringue by heating the honey, the glucose and the rest of the sugar to 120°C (240°F).
• Whip the egg-whites until they are completely firm and add the cooked honey. Mix until it is completely cooled down. Mix the nougatine powder into the meringue. Add the sultanas.
• Add the whipped cream.
• Keep in the deep freeze.

QUINCE TURNOVERS

Serves 4

4 ripe quince
Puff pastry
4 spoons apple compote
1 egg yolk

Syrup
1 litre (2 pints) water
750 g (1.6 lbs) sugar

• Make syrup with 1 litre (2 pints) water and sugar. Cook whole quince, with skin, in syrup. Leave in syrup to cool.
• Meanwhile, prepare 4 rounds of pastry 20 cm (8 inches) in diameter and 3 mm (1/10 inch) thick.
• Dice quince, removing pips but leaving skin.
• Spread compote in middle of pastry and top with diced quince.
• Fold pastry to make turnover and seal with egg yolk.
• Use remaining egg yolk to brush over pastry.
• Prick with fork and bake in an oven preheated to 180°C (360°F).
• Bake for 20 minutes.

I advise you to eat them while warm. They are tastier hot than cold.

LIST OF RECIPES

APPETISERS

Chick pea and paprika dip 6
Tapenade 8
Anchovy fillets marinated in wine 9
Anchovies marinated with lemon
and herbs 10

SOUPS

Soupe au pistou (Pesto Soup) 12
Fish soup 14
Mussel soup with saffron 16
Cream of lentil soup 17

STARTERS

Salt cod brandade with garlic croutons ..18
Game meatballs 20
Herby meatballs 21
Tomato tartare with herbs
and raw shallots 22
Sardine tart with oven-dried tomatoes 24
Savoury chicken liver flan 25

FISH

Red mullet with thick black-olive sauce ..26
Gratin of scorpion fish with potatoes 28
Grilled tuna on a bed of mixed
pan-fried peppers 29
Bouillabaisse ("fish stew") 30
Cuttlefish stuffed with ceps 32
Monkfish tail in breadcrumbs
with its aïoli sauce 33

MEAT DISHES

Rabbit with herbs 34
Saddle of rabbit with pistou 36
Jugged hare 37
Roast partridge with kale chartreuse 38
Leg of duck with ceps 40
Guinea fowl supreme stuffed
with foie gras...41
Roast loin of lamb with courgettes
and tomatoes 42
Daube à l'avignonnaise
(Avigon-style casserole) 44
Trotters and packets 46
Beef cheek 47

VEGETABLES

Provençal tomatoes 48
Round courgettes from Nice stuffed
with fragrant marjoram 50
Ragoût of snow peas and bacon 51
Artichoke barigoule 52
Ratatouille 54

DESSERTS

Pine-Kernel tart 56
Oreillettes ("sweet pastry fritters") 58
Provençal navettes ("bobbins") 59
Croquants ("crunchies") 60
Pompe à huile or fougasse
("sweet flatbread") 62
Iced nougat with honey from Provence ..65
Quince turn overs 66

*Sébastien Merdrignac extends his thanks to ceramic artists
Margot Lhomme and Anne Huet Rapeaud.*

Also by Editions Ouest-France:

Editions OUEST-FRANCE
Lille - Rennes

Éditor Jérôme Le Bihan • Editorial coordination Isabelle Rousseau
Editorial collaboration Lucie Winetz
Graphic design and page layout Studio des Éditions Ouest-France
Photoengraving graph&ti, Cesson-Sévigné (35) • Printing Imprimerie Loire Offset Titoulet, Saint-Etienne (42)
© 2015, Éditions Ouest-France, Édilarge SA, Rennes • ISBN 978-2-7373-6679-6 • Publisher's No. 7783.01.02.04.15
legal deposit: april 2015 • Printed in France • www.editionsouestfrance.fr